The Man, the Boy and the Donkey

Retold and dramatised from the
Aesop's fable as a reading play
for partners or small groups.

Ellie Hallett

Ways to read this story

This story is suitable for school and home. Some 'how to read' ideas are below.

- With a partner or small group, take it in turns to read the rows.

- Don't rush! This helps you to say each word clearly.

- Think of yourselves as actors by adding lots of facial and vocal expression. Small gaps of silence also create dramatic energy. These techniques will bring the story to life.

- If you meet a new word, try to break it down and then say it again. if you have any problems, ask your teacher or a reading buddy.

- Don't be scared of unusual words. They will become your new best friends.
(New words strengthen your general knowledge and enable you to become vocabulary-rich in your day-to-day life.)

Performance note on the ellipsis ...
The ellipsis (three dots ...) in this story shows where the beginning of one speech is said on top of the end of the previous one. And yes — this means two people are speaking at the same time, but it happens in real life.

Note also that capital letters have been used for words that are to be spoken especially loudly.

'I have some sad news, son. We need to sell our donkey at the local market today.'

'Sell our donkey? Why must we do that, Dad? She is almost a member of our family'.

'Come over here so that I can explain to you quietly, son.'

'I can't believe that you want to ...'

'Sh! I want to, well, buy a horse.'

'A horse? But horses are very big and they eat a lot more and ...'

'**Sh**! Keep your voice down, son.

I don't want our donkey to hear what we are saying!'

'But what's wrong with our donkey, Dad? Why must we sell her?'

'She can be very, very stubborn, and she is often moody.'

'She is only stubborn and moody when her load is too heavy ...'

'Yes yes, I know I overload her sometimes. But, but, well, the real reason to sell her is - I think she is too smart for her own good.'

'She is clever enough to tell the time, Dad. She brays at six o'clock every day to wake me for school.'

'The discussion is over, son. We need to get ready to walk to town.'

'Walk to town, Dad? That'll take hours! And the road is dusty ...'

'I want to be at the market in town in time for the early afternoon buyers.'

'Why is that good, Dad?'

'A market man once told me that early afternoon buyers have twice the money and half the sense.'

'Dad, I just saw our donkey smile.'

Later, and on the road to the town.

'Dad! Those travellers are pointing at us and laughing.'

'Ignore them, son. Walk smartly and hold your head high. They may want to buy our donkey.'

'Oh good. That means we can go home.'

The two travellers talk loudly to each other.

'Can you see what I can see, Tim?'

'What are you talking about, Tom?'

'Up ahead, Tim. A silly looking chap and a poor little lad ...'

'Oh yes! And they're walking along with a smart-looking donkey.'

'Excuse me, sir. We travellers need to make a suggestion.'

'That young lad of yours with his thin little legs looks worn out.'

'He should ride the donkey.'

'Perhaps you are right. Thank you for your advice.

Up you get on the donkey, son.'

The two travellers disappear into the distance.

'Hmmm ...' (But I won't tell Dad that our donkey is smiling to herself.)

Half an hour later.

'The road is getting busier, Dad. From up here I can see two smart merchants about to go past.'

'Good morning, merchants. A lovely day for a walk!'

The two merchants talk loudly.

'It *was* a good morning until now.'

'Why are you riding, laddy, while your poor old dad has to walk?'

'I think you need to respect your elders, you selfish young man.'

'Dismount at once and help your old dad up onto the donkey!'

'Hurry up! An elderly gent needs to rest his weary old bones.'

'I'm not elderly, and my bones ...'

'We merchants see things better than most people ...'

'... and we can tell that you are almost on death's door, sir.'

'It must be a terrible thing to have a selfish, good-for-nothing son.'

'My son is a perfectly fine ...'

'May you travel well for your journey. We wish you comfort in your old age. Goodbye!'

The two merchants continue on their way.

'Phew, Dad. What cranky busybodies those merchants were!'

'Fancy them saying I was old!'

'And I'm quite happy to walk.' (I'm sure I saw our donkey smiling again.)

Half an hour later.

'We are making good time, son.'

'Hey Dad - can you hear voices?'

'Yes, I can. Two ladies are coming around the corner up ahead.'

'Hmmm ... They are pointing at us, Dad. What else could be wrong?'

'We have pleased the travellers and pleased the merchants.'

'That means we have nothing to worry about, Dad.'

'And I don't want to have any more stops. We must get to town a s a p.'

The two ladies talk loudly.

'What a selfish man, perched up on his donkey like the king himself.'

'And, what's worse, he is making his dear little boy walk.'

'His tender feet will be ruined! Poor sweet lad. I think I'm going to cry!'

'Hey, you up there! Your majesty! Why is your brave child walking on gravel while you ride in comfort?'

'What a brave little soldier he is, trying his hardest to keep up.'

The two ladies continue on their way, crying loudly.

'What do we do now, Dad? Maybe the ladies are right.'

'Up you get, son. There is only one way to solve this. Both of us will have to ride the donkey to town!'

Half an hour later.

'Dad. Can you move up a bit? I'm about to slide down the donkey's tail and land on the road.'

'And I'm about to slip down the donkey's neck, bounce over her ears and tumble onto the road.'

'We have also slowed down so much that we are barely moving.'

'If it's not one thing, it's another!'

A very large land-owner arrives on a sad little horse.

'Hey! You two silly billies!'

'Your donkey can hardly walk with such a heavy load.'

'I call it cruelty to animals!'

The land-owner gallops off.

'We need to think, son. There must be a way to solve this problem.'

Quite a few minutes later.

'YES! I have it! I know what to do!'

'How can we go to town and, and, and still please everyone, Dad?'

'We'll carry the donkey, son! A clever idea, don't you agree?'

'Carry the donkey? Umm. How will we be able to do that?'

'Look around for a fallen branch and some rope and I'll show you.'

After finding some rope and a branch.

'Tie her front legs together, son, and I'll do the back legs. Now - ready, steady, up we go! LIFT!'

'Whoa! Our donkey is very heavy, Dad! Are you sure this will work?'

'No problem. We'll just make sure she doesn't swing from side to side.'

'Carrying a donkey is unusual, Dad. What will people think?'

'They'll see it as proof of how much we care for animals. And that means we'll get a better price!'

'I hope we are near the town, Dad.

My shoulder is starting to hurt and my feet are getting blisters.'

'Not far now, son. Walk slowly and steadily with your knees bent.'

Thirty minutes later.

'Well, at last! Here we are. And the market is full of people, Dad.'

'That's good, son! And buyers are already admiring our donkey.'

'But Dad. Something odd is happening.'

'What did you say, son?'

'People are coming out of their houses to look at us, Dad!'

'That's a very good sign, son. We have created a seller's market.'

A town crier stands on a box and speaks to the crowd.
'Observe the strangest sight you will see in your whole life, good people!'
'What did you say, Mr Town Crier? I'm a bit deaf. Speak louder!'
'Here before you is a donkey, a fine looking animal, and she is ...'
'I can't see. Stop pushing me, Oscar. I was here first!'
'Yes, ladies and gentlemen. A donkey is being carried on a, oh I can hardly get the words out ...'
'Spit it out, man! I haven't all day!'

'Ha ha ha. This donkey is being carried – by a man and a young lad – ho ho ho - ON A STICK!'

'Quick! My camera, Mandy! I need a picture to show my husband.'

'Yippee! The circus is in town ...!'

'The donkey is now laughing and kicking her hooves ...'

'Hee haw! Hee haw!'

'I haven't had this much fun in years, Sandy!'

'What's happening now, Pete?'

'Well, her front legs are free ...'

'... and yes, down go the back legs, and wow! She's off!'

'Ladies and gentlemen! That clever donkey has escaped. And she seems to be laughing!'

'Down the road she goes and around the corner out of sight. That donkey is smart enough to look after herself.'

'Look, everyone. The owners are sitting in the middle of the road sadly scratching their heads.'

'As Town Crier, I will ask why they were, tee hee, carrying a donkey. I'll then make an announcement.'

'Excuse me for asking, sir, but donkeys normally do the carrying. Why did you think it was better to do it the other way around?'

'Good question!'

'I'm afraid we made a big mistake.'

'We tried to please everyone, but in the end we pleased no-one.'

'And now we have no donkey and no money.'

'As Town Crier, I will announce to everyone in the town that this is a lesson to us all!'

'When you try to please everyone, you will please no-one.'

Postscript: The donkey found a good home with lots of other donkeys, and lived a long and happy life.

After their adventure, the man and the boy made better decisions, and lived a poor but good life.

Some educational outcomes this story format provides

- High-level peer teaching happens without teacher instruction.

- Because the story is in first person, it enables the reader to be **in** the action of the story rather than standing outside and looking in.

- Shy children will forget themselves and unknowingly **become** the characters.

- Children will instinctively add their own creative touches.

- Performing the story for an audience is a valuable confidence booster for all abilities of children, and can provide magic memories that last well beyond the moment.

- The social interaction via body language, facial expression and vocal nuances between readers cannot easily be taught in isolation. When children are involved emotionally, however, these vitally important and life-enriching bonding elements have every chance of occurring spontaneously.